LET'S TALK ABOUT IT

MOVING

Caitie McAneney

PowerKiDS press.

New York

Published in 2015 by The Rosen Publishing Group, Inc.
29 East 21st Street, New York, NY 10010

First Edition

Editor: Caitie McAneney
Book Design: Mickey Harmon

Photo Credits: Cover/series logo Alhovik/Shutterstock.com; cover banner moham'ed/Shutterstock.com; cover image Darren Baker/Shutterstock.com; back cover, pp. 3, 4, 6, 8, 10, 12, 14, 15, 16, 18, 20, 22–24 (interior background) Matyas Szabo/Shutterstock.com; p. 5 Anna Jurkovska/Shutterstock.com; pp. 7, 13, 14, 19, 22 Monkey Business Images/Shutterstock.com; p. 9 Dragon Images/Shutterstock.com; p. 11 Tyler Olsen/Shutterstock.com; p. 15 (kids) Andresr/Shutterstock.com; p. 15 (album) Vasilyev Alexandr/Shutterstock.com; p. 16 Kamira/Shutterstock.com; p.17 Artazum and Iriana Shiyan/Shutterstock.com; pp. 20, 21 Life Photo Studio/Shutterstock.com.

Library of Congress Cataloging-in-Publication Data

McAneney, Caitie.
Moving / by Caitie McAneney.
p. cm. — (Let's talk about it)
Includes index.
ISBN 978-1-4777-5801-4 (pbk.)
ISBN 978-1-4777-5800-7 (6-pack)
ISBN 978-1-4777-5802-1 (library binding)
1. Moving, Household — Juvenile literature. 2. Moving, Household — Psychological aspects — Juvenile literature. 3. Moving, Household — Social aspects — Juvenile literature. I. McAneney, Caitie. II. Title.
TX307.M348 2015
648—d23

Manufactured in the United States of America

CPSIA Compliance Information: Batch #CW15PK: For Further Information contact Rosen Publishing, New York, New York at 1-800-237-9932

CONTENTS

HOME SWEET HOME

A home is more than just a building. It may be the place where you live with your parents, grandparents, or other caregiver. You probably have friends and neighbors nearby. Home is a place where you feel safe and make some of your favorite memories. That's why leaving home can be so hard.

What happens if you find out you have to move to a new home? This news can be hard to hear.

TELL ME MORE

When you first hear bad news, you might be in shock or you might not understand it. Take time to let the news of moving sink in.

You might feel sad, worried, or angry if you find out your friend or family member is moving away, too. Change can be hard to handle.

WHY PEOPLE MOVE

Families have to move for many different reasons. A parent may have gotten a new job in a different city or state. Sometimes a parent loses a job, and a family might have to move somewhere more affordable.

Other times, a family moves to be closer to things they value. They may want to move closer to a better school or a safer community. Maybe your family is moving closer to other family members. Sometimes people move closer to grandparents and family members who need help.

TELL ME MORE

Understanding why you're moving might make you feel better. Talk to your parents about their reasons and try to keep an open mind.

Parents usually decide to move because it's best for the whole family. It might seem unfair now, but moving could be the best choice for the future.

OPENING UP

Even if you understand why you're moving, you may still feel badly. It's okay to feel worried or sad. You might be sad about leaving your friends and worried they'll forget you. You might worry that you won't make new friends in your new school and neighborhood.

Open up to someone about your feelings. Talking to a parent, family member, or friend can help you feel better. They might have advice on what to do. They might tell you that they're feeling sad and worried, too.

The people you can talk to are called your support system. Opening up to them might make you feel like you're not the only one who's worried or sad.

9

LOOKING INTO IT

Finding out more about your new home might help you feel better about moving there. Can you find it on a map? Maybe it's not as far away as you thought. Maybe it's right near a playground or **museum**.

You can ask your family what they know about the new place. If it's far away, you can ask what the **climate** and surroundings are like. You can use the Internet to **research** things around your new community. Is there a great library or skating rink nearby?

Finding out more about your new community can help you get excited. You may feel better knowing you don't have to give up your favorite hobbies.

PACKING

Seeing your things packed into boxes can be tough. What can you do before packing to feel better?

You can take pictures of your home before you pack. This will help you always remember what it looked like. Next, you can pack a special box to help you feel better when you move. Fill the box with your favorite things, such as posters and toys. Mark it with your name so you know exactly where it is when you get to your new place.

TELL ME MORE

The first few nights in a new home can be strange. Make sure to pack a bag with all the things you might need the first night—especially a toothbrush!

It may feel like you have no control over moving. But you do have control over getting your own belongings ready.

13

SAYING GOODBYE

One of the hardest parts of moving is saying goodbye to your friends. You may be scared that your friendships will change.

Remember that just because your friendships may change, that doesn't mean you'll lose them.

Before you say goodbye, make plans to see your friends again. If you're not moving far, make plans to have them over for a party or a sleepover. If you're moving farther, make plans to video chat or talk on the phone. Get their addresses and phone numbers so they're only a letter, e-mail, or phone call away!

TELL ME MORE

You can take lots of pictures with your friends before you leave. Then, you can put the pictures in your new home so you'll always remember them!

A NEW PLACE

Your new place will probably feel weird for a little while. It may look empty and not like "home." Give yourself time to get used to your new place. Your other family members, even your parents, might be uneasy or worried, too. It's normal to miss your old home.

At first, it may seem like you have no control over your surroundings, but you do! Make your new room your own. If you share a room, you can **decorate** your side just the way you like.

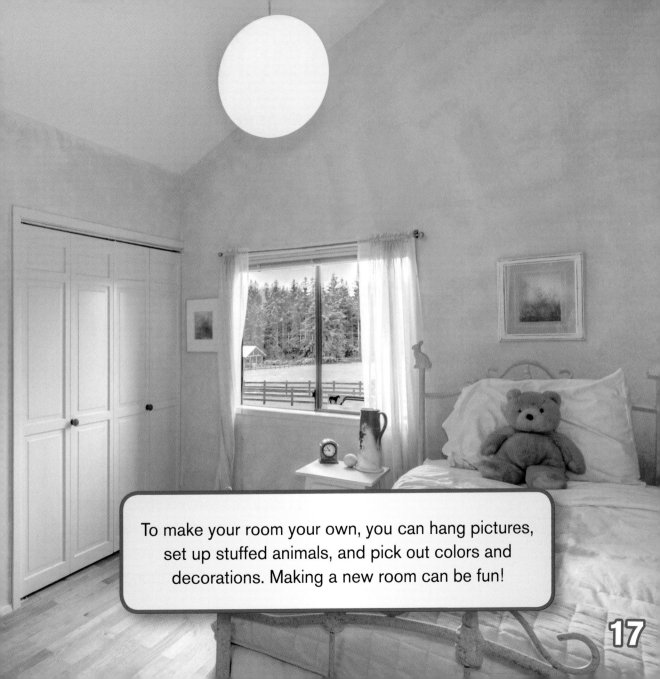

To make your room your own, you can hang pictures, set up stuffed animals, and pick out colors and decorations. Making a new room can be fun!

17

STARTING SCHOOL

It's not easy to be the new kid at school. It can be hard to make new friends and find your way around. It'll take a while to settle in, but there are things you can do to make that easier.

Find out if there are clubs and teams you can join. This will help you meet new people, and it will keep you busy. Many schools have clubs for art, **volunteering**, or science. There are likely sports teams, too, such as basketball and baseball.

TELL ME MORE

You may be worried about getting lost around the school. Ask for a tour of the school so you can get an idea of where things are.

If your new classes seem tough, don't be afraid to ask your teacher for help.

19

AROUND THE COMMUNITY

If you didn't move far, you may live in the same community you grew up in. In that case, you can still visit your favorite places, such as the library and park. But if you've moved farther away, you'll have a whole new community to **explore**.

Explore your neighborhood with your parents. You can visit your new park, stores, and restaurants. If you see other kids outside, **introduce** yourself. Being friendly and open to meeting new people will help you settle in to your new community.

Many communities have fun programs and classes for kids. You can join a dance **studio**, community football team, or swim class.

21

IS IT HOME YET?

It can take a while for your new house or apartment to feel like a home. It's okay if it doesn't happen right away. The more you decorate, meet new friends, and make new memories, the more it'll start to feel like "yours."

It's healthy to talk about your feelings after the move. You may cry and miss your old home. You may get angry that you had to leave. Be **patient** with your feelings. One day, your new house or apartment will feel just like home.

GLOSSARY

climate: The common weather in a place.

decorate: To add objects that make something prettier or more interesting.

explore: To search something to find out more about it.

introduce: To make someone known by name to another person.

museum: A place where art or historical pieces are safely kept for people to see and to study.

patient: Waiting calmly for something.

research: To study something carefully to find out more about it.

studio: A place to study dancing, singing, or art.

volunteer: To do something to help because you want to do it.

INDEX

WEBSITES

Due to the changing nature of Internet links, PowerKids Press has developed an online list of websites related to the subject of this book. This site is updated regularly. Please use this link to access the list: www.powerkidslinks.com/ltai/mov